What is . . . ?

What is grey and furry and goes up and down?
A mouse in a lift.

What is grey and furry, dries quickly, and needs no ironing?
A drip-dry mouse.

What is a mouse's least favourite newspaper?
Mews of the World.

What is grey and furry and hums?
An electric mouse.

What is grey and furry and goes bang, bang, bang, bang.
A four-door mouse.

What is small, blue and furry?
A mouse holding it's breath.

What is grey and furry and bounces?
A mouse on a pogo stick.

'What is your favourite colour?'
'Red'.
'And what is your favourite animal?'
'A mouse.'
'And what is your favourite number?'
'Seven.'
'So when did you last see a red mouse with seven legs . . . ?'

What is grey and furry and goes at 125 m.p.h.?
A mouse on an Inter-City train.

What is grey and furry and goes round and round?
A mouse in a revolving door.

What is grey and furry and has eight wheels?
A mouse on roller skates.

What is small, green, and eats cheese?
An unripe mouse.

What is grey on the inside, and green on the outside?
A mouse disguised as a cucumber.

What is red and grey on the outside, and grey and furry on the inside?
An inside-out mouse.

What is grey and red and goes round and round very fast?
A mouse in a food processor.

What is a nouse?
The one after a mouse.

What is mouse skin used for most?
To keep mice together.

What is grey and furry and carries malaria?
A mousequito.

What is grey and furry and lives under the sea?
A mouse with an aqualung.

What is a mouse after it is four days old?
Five days old.

What is the first thing a mouse does in the morning?
It wakes up.

This copy of

A VERY MICE JOKE BOOK

belongs to

....

—A—
VERY MICE
JOKE BOOK

John Hegarty
Illustrated by Mark Burgess

Beaver Books

A Beaver Book
Published by Arrow Books Limited
62–5 Chandos Place, London WC2N 4NW

An imprint of Century Hutchinson Ltd

London Melbourne Sydney Auckland
Johannesburg and agencies throughout the world

First published 1986

Set in Century Schoolbook
by JH Graphics Ltd, Reading, Berks.

Made and printed in Great Britain
by Anchor Brendon Ltd
Tiptree, Essex

ISBN 0 09 948160 X

For Louise Rose,
my very special little mouse

Contents

What is grey and furry and travels behind the skirting board at 100 m.p.h.?
A mouse on a motorbike.

What is the best way to keep mice from smelling?
Cut off their noses.

What is grey and has a trunk?
A mouse going on holiday.

What is a mouse's least favourite TV programme?
Mews at Ten.

What is grey and furry and noisy?
A mouse with a drum set.

What is grey and furry and weighs 90 pounds?
A fat mouse.

What is big, grey and furry and lives in a Scottish lake?
The Loch Ness mouse.

What is grey and furry, with red spots?
A mouse with measles.

What is the best way to get a wild mouse?
Buy a tame one and irritate it.

What is the hardest part of milking a mouse?
Getting the bucket under it.

What is a cat's favourite TV programme?
Miami Mice.

What is it called when a gang of mice put on disguises and have a party?
A mousquerade.

What is a well-known mouse called?
Famouse!

What is grey and hairy and lives on a man's face?
A moustache.

What is it called when a lot of Red Indians have a battle with a few mice?
A mousacre.

What is the mouse word for a tandem?
A micycle.

What do get if . . . ?

What do you get if you cross a mouse with an elephant?
Dirty great holes in the skirting board.

What do you get if you cross a mouse with peanut butter?
A mouse that sticks to the roof of your mouth.

What do you get if you cross a mouse with a Chinese president?
Mouse Tse Tung.

What do you get if you cross five legs, two tails and 1000 whiskers?
A mouse with spare parts.

What do you get if you cross a mouse with a boy scout?
A mouse that helps old ladies cross the road.

What do you get if you cross a mouse with potatoes and cabbage?
Bubble and squeak.

What do you get if you cross a mouse with an alleyway?
A narrow squeak.

What do you get if you cross a mouse with an orange?
A pip squeak.

What do you get if you cross a mouse with a Greek singer?
Nana Mousekouri.

What do you get if you cross a mouse with a gorilla?
I don't know – but if it squeaks, you'd better smile!

What do you get if you cross a river with an inflatable mouse?
To the other side.

What do you get if you cross a mouse and a monkey?
A swinging mouse.

What do you get if you cross an elephant with a mouse?
Mighty Mouse.

What do you get if you cross a mouse with a shipping beacon?
A lightmouse.

What do you get if you cross a mouse with a drinking establishment?
A public mouse.

What do you get if you cross a mouse with a lion?
A mouse that cats leave alone.

What do you get if you cross a mouse with a Cornetto?
Mice cream.

What do you get if you cross a mouse with hair on your lip?
A mousetache.

What do you get if you cross a mouse with a Hoover and an iron?
Mousework.

What do you do . . . ?

What do you do if you hear a mouse squeaking?
Oil it.

What does a mouse do when it's raining?
Gets wet.

What do you do if you find 1000 mice in your bed?
Sleep somewhere else.

How . . . ?

How can you tell an Italian mouse from a Scottish one?
By its suntan.

How do you keep a mouse from eating your Sunday lunch?
Trap him on Saturday.

How can you tell an apple from a mouse?
If it's red it's probably an apple.

How do you pick up a mouse that has been crossed with a porcupine?
Very carefully.

How can you stop a mouse from squeaking in your bedroom?
Put it in the kitchen.

How are a mouse and a penny alike?
Both have a head and a tail.

How can you tell a mouse from spaghetti?
A mouse doesn't slip off the end of your fork.

How long should a mouse's legs be?
Long enough to reach the ground.

'How is a mouse like a grape?'
'I don't know.'
'They're both purple – except for the mouse.'

How did the Egyptian mouse catch a cold?
It caught it from its mummy.

How do you get a mouse in a box of matches?
Take the matches out first.

How well did the mouse get on with other mice?
Like a mouse on fire!

How do you spell mousetrap in three letters?
C-A-T.

How do you catch a mouse?
Make a noise like a piece of cheese.

How do you get 10,000 mice in a Mini?
5000 in the front, and 5000 in the back.

How do you get an elephant into a Mini?
You can't. It's full up with mice.

How do you make a mouse stew?
Keep it waiting for three hours.

How do you make a mouse float?
Take two scoops of ice cream and add one mouse.

How do male and female mice find each other in the dark?
Delightful.

How can you tell if you have a mouse in bed with you?
By the 'M' embroidered on its pyjamas.

How many mice in a hammerfor?
What's a hammerfor?
Banging in nails!

How do you get 10,000 mice into a phone box?
Open the door.

How do mice dive into swimming pools?
Head first.

How do you save a drowning mouse?
Give it mouse-to-mouse resuscitation.

*How does a cat feel when it's chased all the mice
out of the house?*
Mouse proud.

How do you make a thin mouse fat?
Throw it off a cliff and it will come down
'PLUMP!'

Why . . . ?

Why do the mice in Toyland have Big Ears?
Because Noddy won't pay the ransom.

Why don't mice eat Penguins?
Because they can't get the wrappers off.

Why does a mouse wear yellow socks?
Because the grey ones are at the laundry.

Why did the mouse stop tap dancing?
Because it fell into the sink.

Why does a mouse wear sandals?
To go to the beach.

Why do elephants have corrugated feet?
To give the mice a fifty-fifty chance.

*Why did the mouse paint the soles of its feet
yellow?*
So it could hide upside down in a bowl of custard.

Why do mice lie down at night?
Because they can't lie up.

Why didn't the mouse hurt itself when it fell off a tall ladder?
It only fell from the bottom rung.

Why did the mouse paint itself 20 different colours?
So it could hide in a crayon box.

Why did the mouse cross the road?
It was the chicken's day off.

Why is it dangerous to put the letter 'M' into the fridge?
Because it changes ice into mice.

Why is a mousetrap like the measles?
Because it's catching.

Why did the mouse climb Nelson's Column?
To get its kite.

Why did the mouse go over the mountain?
It couldn't go under it.

Why wasn't the lost mouse ad. in the paper any good?
Mice never read newspapers.

Why are mice such gossips?
They always carry tails with them.

Why is a mouse grey and furry?
So you can tell it from an aspirin.

Why don't mice ride bicycles?
They don't have a thumb to ring the bell with.

Why are mice poor dancers?
They have two left feet.

Why was the mouse so small?
Someone fed it condensed milk.

Why do mice wear green felt hats?
So they can walk across snooker tables without being seen.

Why do mice wear slippers?
So they can walk around without cats hearing them.

Why do mice scratch themselves?
They're the only ones that know where they itch.

Why does an elephant have a trunk?
So that he has somewhere to hide if he sees a mouse.

Why did the mouse dye its hair yellow?
To see if blondes have more fun.

Why do mice have grey fur coats?
They'd look odd in tweed ones.

MOTHER MOUSE: *Johnny, there were two lumps of cheese in the larder yesterday, and now there's only one. Why?*

JOHNNY: I don't know, Mum, It must have been so dark I didn't see the second one.

Why did the mouse nibble a hole in the carpet?
Because it wanted to see the floor show.

Why aren't mice big, white and shiny?
If they were, they'd be fridges.

'Why are you spreading that powder around?'
'To keep mice away.'
'But there aren't any mice around here.'
'Good stuff, isn't it?'

*'The police are looking for an escaped pet mouse
with one eye.'*
'Why don't they use two?'

*Why did the king mouse wear red, white and blue
braces?*
To keep his trousers up.

Why is a mouse in the desert like Christmas?
Because of its sandy claws.

Why is a mouse's nose in the middle of its face?
Because it's the scenter.

Why did the mouse have her hair in a bun?
Because she had her nose in a cheeseburger.

*Why does a mouse with its eyes closed resemble a
bad schoolteacher?*
Because it keeps its pupils in darkness.

Why did Freddie put a frog in his sister's bed?
Because he couldn't catch a mouse.

Why did the mouse cross the road?
Because it was stapled to the chicken. (Ugh!)

Why is a mouse in the desert like Christmas?
Because of its sandy claws.

Why do cats eat cheese?
So they can breathe down mouseholes with baited breath.

When . . . ?

What did they say?

When should a mouse carry an umbrella?
When it's raining cats and dogs.

When do mice have eight feet?
When there are two of them.

When was the coldest part of history, for mice?
The mice age.

When did the mouse on the Titanic start screaming?
When it saw the miceberg.

When are Torvill and Dean most popular with mice?
When they are mice skating.

What did they say . . . ?

What did the mouse say when the farmer's wife grabbed it by the tail?
'That is the end of me.'

What did the grey mouse say to the blue mouse?
'Cheer up.'

What did the man say when he saw 1000 mice come over the hill?
'Here come the mice.'

What did his wife say?
'Here come the gooseberries.' (She was colour blind.)

What did the man say when he saw 1000 mice wearing sunglasses come over the hill?
Nothing. He didn't recognize them.

What did the cheese say to the mouse?
Nothing. Cheese can't talk.

What did the mouse say when it ate a reel of film?
'The book was better.'

50 mice were standing in single file, all facing the same way. How many of them could say, 'My nose is touching another mouse's tail?'
None. Mice can't speak.

What did the dog say to the mouse?
'Woof Woof.'

What did the American mouse say to the other American mouse?
'Have a mice day.'

What did the mouse say when it only had thistles to eat?
'Thistle have to do.'

*What did the two ton mouse say when it walked
into the alley?*
'Here, kitty, kitty, kitty.'

*What did the mouse say when it broke two of its
front teeth?*
'Hard cheese.'

Where . . . ?

Where would the U.S. President live if he was a mouse?
In the White Mouse.

Where would the Prime Minister speak if she was a mouse?
In the Mouse of Commons.

Where do mice go skating?
At a mice rink.

Where do mice live in Hong Kong?
On a mouseboat.

Where do mice go to celebrate their new house?
To a mouse-warming party.

Where do you find wild mice?
It depends where you lost them.

FIRST MOUSE: *Where do you sleep?*
SECOND MOUSE: On a chandelier.
FIRST MOUSE: *Why's that?*
SECOND MOUSE: Because I'm a light sleeper.

Where does a two ton mouse sit when it goes to the theatre?
Anywhere it wants to!

FIRST ESKIMO MOUSE: *Where does your mother come from?*
SECOND ESKIMO MOUSE: Alaska.
FIRST ESKIMO MOUSE: *Don't bother. I'll ask her myself.*

What's the difference . . . ?

What's the difference between a mouse and an apple?
Have you ever tried peeling a mouse?

What's the difference between a mouse and a grapefruit?
A mouse is grey.

What's the difference between a mouse and a flea?
A mouse can have fleas, but a flea can't have mice.

What's the difference between a mouse and a comma?
A mouse has claws at the end of its paws, a comma has a pause at the end of its clause.

What's the difference between a mouse and a biscuit?
Ever tried dunking a mouse in your tea?

What's the difference between a mouse and an egg?
Ever tried scrambling a mouse?

What's the difference between a mouse and an elephant?
Try picking them up. An elephant is usually heavier.

What's the difference between a riddle and two mice sitting on a bun?
One is a conundrum and the other is a bununder'em.

What . . . ?

What species of mouse weighs 2000 pounds?
The hippopotamouse.

What do cats eat for breakfast?
Mice Krispies.

What species of mouse weighs 2000 pounds and wears a flower behind its ear?
A hippypotamouse.

What do mice have that no other animal has?
Baby mice.

What animal has a grey fur coat and is found at the North Pole?
A very lost mouse.

What should a mouse do if it's chased by an elephant?
Make a trunk call and reverse the charge.

What do you need to write an essay on a mouse?
Find yourself a small pen, a magnifying glass,
and something to keep the mouse still while
you're writing on it. . . !

*What kinds of mice have their eyes closest
together?*
The smallest ones.

What has four legs and flies?
A dead mouse.

What can a mouse do that an elephant can't?
Take a bath in a saucer.

What kind of mouse eats with its tail?
They all do. They also sleep with them.

*What do angry mice send to each other at
Yuletide?*
Crossmouse cards.

What goes ha, ha, ha, clunk?
A mouse laughing its head off.

What looks like half a lump of cheese?
The other half.

Why did the mice rush out of the chemist's?
Because there was a puss in Boots.

What animal is a mouse like when it takes a bath?
A little bear.

What do you call a cat burglar who steals mice?
A mousebreaker.

What do cats like eating at the cinema?
Choc-mice.

What do cats like eating on hot days?
Mice lollies.

What game do mice play in America, on skates?
Mice hockey.

What hang down in mouseholes in the winter?
Micicles.

What brings baby mice?
The stork.

What goes pitter, patter, squelch, squelch?
A mouse with soggy plimsolls.

What side of a mouse has the most fur?
The outside.

*What lives behind the skirting board and is
highly dangerous?*
A mouse with a machine gun.

What do you call a mouse with a machine gun?
Sir.

What usually runs in the mouse family?
Noses.

What animal goes hunting mice in the sea?
A catfish.

If cheese comes after dinner, what comes after cheese?
Mice.

What happened to the mouse who listened to a match?
It burnt its ear.

What goes squeak, squeak, bang?
A mouse in a minefield.

What do you call a male mouse with eight children?
Daddy.

What does a mouse do for a light meal?
Eats a candle.

What would you do if you found a mouse chewing your favourite book?
Take the words right out of his mouth.

What should you do if you wake up in the middle of the night and hear a mouse squeaking?
Oil it.

What do you call a mouse that rides first class in a jumbo-jet?
A passenger.

What do you call a mouse that has written a book?
An author.

'*What eats cheese, hides from cats, and is made of cement?*'
'What?'
'*A mouse.*'
'But what about the cement?'
'*I just threw that in to make it hard!*'

What has antlers and eats cheese?
Mickey Moose.

What goes dot, dot, dash, squeak?
Mouse code.

What does a mouse turn into when the lights go out?
The dark.

What makes more noise than an angry mouse?
Two angry mice.

What place of business helps mice who have lost their tails?
A retail shop.

What animals should carry an oilcan?
Mice. They squeak.

What eats cheese and sees as well from either end?
A mouse with its eyes shut.

What would you call a small brown mouse in Russia if it was five days old and had a black spot on the end of its nose?
A baby.

What has four legs but can't walk?
A dead mouse.

What must a mouse be to receive a state funeral?
Dead.

What kinds of mice can jump higher than a house?
All kinds. Houses can't jump.

What has eight legs but can't walk?
Two dead mice.

What does a mouse do when it rains?
Gets wet.

What sort of fur do you get from a giant mouse?
As fur away as possible.

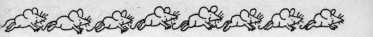

What do you have to know to teach a mouse tricks?
More than the mouse.

What loves cheese, weighs a ton, and lived a million years ago?
A moustadon.

What do powerful mice have on their arms.
Mouscles.

What do you call a mouse that no one's heard of?
Anonymouse.

What do you get if you cross a mouse with an animal with a big bottom?
A hippobottomouse!

What did the little mouse say to the grandfather clock?
'Hello, old timer.'

What do you call bouncers at a mouse disco?
Doormice

Doctor Doctor . . . ?

MOUSE: *Doctor, I'm only two inches tall.*
DOCTOR: You'll just have to be a little patient.

MOUSE: *Doctor, all the other mice think I'm*
              mad.
DOCTOR: Why is that?
MOUSE: *I like sausages.*
DOCTOR: There's nothing strange about that. I
              like sausages too.
MOUSE: *Really? You must come and see my*
              collection then. I've got thousands.

MOUSE: *I keep seeing red spots in front of my eyes.*
DOCTOR: Have you seen a psychiatrist?
MOUSE: *No, just red spots.*

A boy with a mouse on his head went to see a doctor. The doctor said, 'Gosh. You really need help.'
'You said it,' the mouse cried. 'Get this kid out from under me!'

MOUSE: *Doctor, I think I'm a bird.*
DOCTOR: Just perch yourself there and I'll tweet you in a minute.

'Doctor,' said the panic-stricken woman, 'my husband was asleep with his mouth open and he's swallowed a mouse. What shall I do?'
'Quite simple,' said the doctor. 'You just tie a lump of cheese to a piece of string and lower it into your husband's mouth. As soon as the mouse appears and takes a bite – pull him out.'
'Thank you, doctor,' said the woman. 'I'll go round to the fishmonger straight away and get a cod's head.'

'What on earth do you want a cod's head for?'
'Oh, I forgot to tell you. I've got to get the cat out first!'

LADY: *Doctor, doctor, my husband thinks he's a cat.*
DOCTOR: Well what do you want me to do about it?
LADY: *Just stop him eating mice.*

Mouse Talk . . . ?

MOUSE TEACHER: *Now, John, what is the highest form of animal life?*

MOUSE PUPIL: The giraffe.

MOUSE TEACHER: *Name four members of the cat family?*

MOUSE PUPIL: Mummy cat, Daddy cat, and two kittens.

KID MOUSE:	*Mum, am I made of sage and onion?*
MOTHER MOUSE:	Of course not. Why?
KID MOUSE:	*Because a big mouse from the end of the street said he's going to knock the stuffing out of me.*

MOUSE TEACHER:	*This essay on 'My House' is exactly the same as your brother's.*
MOUSE PUPIL:	Well, it's the same house.

FIRST MOUSE:	*My Dad made a bad mistake today, and chewed through a packet of soapflakes instead of cornflakes.*
SECOND MOUSE:	Was he cross?
FIRST MOUSE:	*He foamed at the mouth.*

MOUSE TEACHER:	*What is a skeleton?*
MOUSE PUPIL:	It's a mouse with his outsides off and his insides out.

MOTHER MOUSE (to older son):	*Why is your little brother crying?*
SON:	Because I won't give him my piece of cheese.
MOTHER MOUSE:	*Is his piece gone?*
SON:	Yes. He cried when I ate it, too.

FIRST MOUSE:	*What a terrible bump on your head. How did you get that?*
SECOND MOUSE:	Some tomatoes fell on my head.
FIRST MOUSE:	*Tomatoes! How could tomatoes cause such a huge bump?*
SECOND MOUSE:	They were in a tin.

FIRST MOUSE:	*I've been hunting with my Dad. We brought back four lumps of cheese and a potfer.*
SECOND MOUSE:	What's a potfer?
FIRST MOUSE:	*To cook the cheese in.*

SMART MOUSE: *Can you spell blind mice?*
DIM MOUSE: B-l-i-n-d m-i-c-e.
SMART MOUSE: *No, it's b-l-n-d m-c-e. With two i's they wouldn't be blind.*

FIRST THIN MOUSE: *Will you join me in a ginger beer?*
SECOND FAT MOUSE: Sorry, the bottle's just too thin for me.

FIRST MOUSE: *Do you know the quickest way to the station?*
SECOND MOUSE: Yes – run.

Two mice, walking in opposite directions, met in a country lane. 'Squeak, squeak!' said the first mouse.
'Hee-haw!' said the second.
'Squeak, squeak!' said the first again, very surprised.
'Hee-haw!' repeated the second.
'What are you up to?' asked the first mouse. 'Mice don't go hee-haw.'
'Ah, but I'm a stranger round here,' said the second.

| FIRST MOUSE: | *What's your new house like?* |
| SECOND MOUSE: | Oh, it's all right, I suppose. But my bedroom's cold and small – and every time I open the door the light goes on . . . |

| FIRST MOUSE: | *It's raining cats and dogs.* |
| SECOND MOUSE: | I know, I just trod in a poodle. |

| LITTLE MOUSE: | *Mummy, I don't like cheese with holes.* |
| MUMMY MOUSE: | Well just eat the cheese, dear, and leave the holes on the side of your plate. |

'I finally got that stupid scientist trained,' said one mouse to the other in the research laboratory. 'Every time I'm hungry I go to the end of the maze, ring the bell, and he fetches me something to eat.'

The longest little mouse tails in the world . . . ?

'I have an act I think you could use,' said the man
to the TV producer. Out of one pocket he took a
mouse and a miniature piano, which he placed
on the producer's desk. Out of the other he took a
beautiful butterfly. At once the mouse began to
play the piano and the butterfly began to sing.
'That is absolutely sensational,' cried the TV
producer. 'Name your price.'

'There is one thing you should know,' said the
man. 'The act really isn't as good as it seems. You
see, the mouse is a ventriloquist.'

A woman walked into a pet shop and asked for
200 mice.
'What do you want them for?' asked the pet shop
owner.
'My landlord's given me notice to quit,' said the
woman, 'and he says I've got to leave the place
just as I found it.'

A policeman stopped a man who was walking
down the street with a mouse in his hand and
ordered him to take it to the zoo at once. The next
day the policeman saw the man again, still with
the mouse in his hand. 'I thought I told you to
take it to the zoo,' he said.
'I did,' said the man, 'and now I'm taking it to the
pictures.'

A man walked into the police station and put a
dead mouse on the counter. 'Somebody threw
this into my house,' he complained.
'Right, sir,' said the police sergeant, 'if you come
back in six months and no one's claimed it, it's
yours.'

A mouse went into a music shop, jumped on to
the counter, and said to the astonished owner,
'Can I have a mouth organ, please?'

The owner gulped and said, 'This is amazing. Forty years I've been here, and no mouse has ever asked for a mouth organ until today – and you are the second. There was another mouse in here just a few minutes ago, and she asked for a mouth organ, too.'

'Ah yes,' said the mouse, 'that'll be our Monica.'

A Scotsman was paying his first visit to a zoo, when he stopped by one of the cages. 'An' whut animal would that be?' he asked the keeper.

'That's a moose, sir,' came the reply, 'from Canada.'

'A moose!' exclaimed the Scotsman. 'Hoots mon – they must ha' rats like elephants over there.'

All the animals in the jungle had formed themselves into football teams and were playing in a grand knock-out competition to decide the champions. The final match was between the

elephants and the mice, with thousands of
animals from miles around in the crowd.
It was a tough game, with the score at three-all,
and just five minutes left for play. Suddenly the
mouse centre-forward went zooming down the
middle, and looked certain to score. The
elephant sweeper roared in to intercept him, and
squashed the poor creature as flat as a pancake.
The ref. blew his whistle and came running over.
'You've killed him' he said to the elephant. 'That
means a penalty – and I'll have to send you off.'
'But ref.,' pleaded the elephant, 'I didn't mean to
kill him. I only meant to trip him up.'

A mouse walked into a coffee bar and ordered a
cup of coffee. The man behind the counter was
flabbergasted but brought the coffee right away.
The mouse drank its coffee in silence and then
handed the man a five pound note and the man,
thinking the mouse would know nothing about
money, only gave him one pound back in change.
'I hope you enjoyed the coffee,' he said to the
mouse. 'We don't get many mice in here, you
know.'
'Stone me,' said the mouse, 'at four pounds a cup,
I'm not surprised.'

An American was visiting Australia. 'Don't you think that bridge is beautiful?' asked his host. 'Well yes,' said the American, 'but we've got bigger bridges than that back home.'
'What about this park?' asked the Australian, 'Have you ever seen anything like it before?'
'I sure have,' said the American. 'We've got lots of parks bigger than this back home.'
They walked on a bit, until they came to a river. Suddenly they saw a duck-billed platypus running along the bank. 'Well,' said the American, 'one thing I'll have to admit – your mice are a little larger than ours.'

There was a lion who wanted to find out why none of the other animals were as handsome and

strong as he was. First he asked a giraffe; the giraffe didn't know. Next he asked a zebra; the zebra didn't know. Next he asked a hippo; the hippo didn't know. Next he asked a rhino; the rhino didn't know. Finally the lion came across a little mouse. He looked down at the mouse and said, 'Tell me, little mouse, why aren't you as handsome and as strong and as big and as beautiful as I am?'
The little mouse looked up at the lion and said, 'Well, I've not been very well lately.'

A lady was walking down the street carrying a small box with holes punched in the top.
'What's in there?' a friend asked.
'A cat,' the lady replied.
'What for?'
'I've been dreaming about mice at night. The cat is to catch them.'
'But the mice you dream about are imaginary,' said her friend.
'Ah yes,' replied the lady, 'but so is the cat.'

A man went into the police station one day and said that he wanted to make a complaint. 'I've got three brothers,' he explained, 'and we all live

in one room. One of my brothers has six dogs, another has six cats, and the other has a goat. The smell in there is terrible. You must do something.'

'Hasn't your room got any windows?' asked the sergeant.

'Of course it has,' said the man.

'So why don't you open them?' said the policeman.

'What,' said the man, 'and lose all my mice?'

'I had a terrible shock yesterday with my little mouse,' said a man.

'What happened?' his friend asked.

'Well I filled my cigarette lighter just before letting him out of his cage for his exercise, and I must have spilled some of it on the sideboard. Before I could stop him, my mouse had jumped up there and taken a good long slurp.'

'What happened?'

'Well, he gave a sort of strangled squeak, ran straight at the wall, flew up it, banged his head on the ceiling, leapt on to the chandelier, and dropped to the floor. Then he zoomed twice round the room getting faster and faster, into the kitchen, back into the lounge, up the stairs and into the bathroom. He ran straight into the

mirror, bonked his head against the glass and fell into the wash-basin. Then he just lay there, not moving.'
'Was he dead?'
'No, he'd just run out of petrol.'

The absent minded science teacher brought a parcel into the class. 'I caught a mouse, a shrew and a rat yesterday,' he said. 'I want to give you a test, to see if you can tell which is which.'
But when he opened the parcel he took out three sausage rolls. 'Oh my goodness!' he exclaimed. 'What did I eat for my lunch, then?'

A man was out walking in the woods one day when he spotted a very strange looking creature. It seemed to be half squirrel and half mouse. He ran home as fast as he could, picked up the

phone, dialled, and waited, and waited, and waited. Finally, he called the operator, and demanded, 'Why can't I get through to the zoo?' 'Sorry, sir,' said the operator. 'Lion's out of order.'

A man paid a lot of money for a talking mouse. He took it home to show a friend, who offered him 100-1 it wouldn't say a word.
'Right,' said the owner, and did everything he could to make the mouse talk, but nothing happened. So his friend roared with laughter, pocketed the money and left.
The owner turned angrily to the mouse, 'You stupid animal, why didn't you say something?'
'Oi, not so much of the stupid,' replied the mouse. 'Think of the odds we'll get next time!'

Cat and mouse . . . !

'My cat took first prize at the Pet Show,'
'Your cat took first prize at the Pet Show? How
did it manage that?'
'It ate the prize mouse?'

SMART KID: *How far can a cat chase a mouse
into a house.*

FRIEND: I suppose it depends on how big
the house is.

SMART KID: *Oh no it doesn't. A cat can only
chase a mouse halfway into a
house. After that, he's chasing it
out.'*

'I'm very sorry, lady, but I've just run over your cat. I'd like to replace it.'
'How are you at catching mice?'

'I've come to collect the reward for returning your pet mouse.'
'But that's not a mouse – it's a cat.'
'I know. The mouse is inside it.'

'You told me this cat was splendid for mice, but, in two weeks, it hasn't caught a single one.'
'Well, isn't that splendid for mice?'

'When is it bad luck to have a black cat cross your path?
When you are a mouse.

FIRST MOUSE: *What do you call a cat that has just swallowed a duck?*
SECOND MOUSE: Dunno. What *do* you call it?
FIRST MOUSE: *A duck-filled fatty-puss.*

MOUSE (to
pet shop owner):   *Have you any cats going
                      cheap?*
PET SHOP OWNER: Sorry, mate, all cats go
                      miaow.

FIRST MOUSE: *I hear your cat did well in
                      the milk-drinking contest?*
SECOND MOUSE: Yes, it won by four laps.

FIRST MOUSE: *The people in your house
                      just put the cat out.*
SECOND MOUSE: Why, was it on fire?

Where does a mouse list all its enemies?
In a catalogue.

Very mice poems . . . .

Hickory Dickory Dock,
Three mice ran up the clock,
The clock struck one,
And the other two escaped with minor injuries.

Hickory Dickory Dock,
The elephant ran up the clock,
The clock is being repaired.

There once was a mouse of Calcutta,
Who spoke with a terrible stutter.
At breakfast he said,
'Give me b-b-b-bread,
And b-b-b-b-b-b-butter.'

There was a young mouse from the city,
Who saw what he thought was a kitty.
To make sure of that
He gave it a pat.
They buried his clothes – what a pity.

Mary had a little mouse,
It had a touch of colic.
She gave it brandy twice a day –
And now it's alcoholic.

A gentleman dining at Crewe
Found a rather large mouse in his stew.
Said the waiter, 'Don't shout,
Or wave it about,
Or the rest will be wanting one, too.'

Tail pieces . . . .

FRED: *I had to have my pet mouse put down.*
BERT: Was he mad?
FRED: *Well, he wasn't pleased.*

Two mice were playing football in a saucer.
'We'll have to play better than we are at the
moment,' said one of them. 'We're playing in the
cup next week.'

MAN: *I'd like some mouse poison,*
please.
SHOP ASSISTANT: Have you tried Boots?
MAN: *I want to poison them, not*
kick them to death.

Did you hear about the loony fisherman? He baited his hook with rubber mice because he wanted to catch catfish.

Did you ever see the Catskill Mountains?
No, but I've seen them kill mice.

Squeak up. Are you a man or a mouse?

FRED: *Last week I was thrown out of the zoo for feeding the mice.*
BERT: What's so bad about that?
FRED: *I was feeding them to the lions.*

Who is safe when a man-eating mouse is loose?
Women and children.

Is it better to have a tiger eat you, or a mouse?
It's better to have him eat the mouse.

A big, three-legged mouse kicks open the saloon door in an old Wild West town. Guns blazing, he drawls to the packed bar, 'Ah've come for ma paw. . . .'

When ten mice fall into a lake, what is the first thing they do?
Get wet.

If you saw nine mice sitting at the cinema with red socks on, and one mouse with yellow socks on, what would this prove?
That nine out of ten mice wear red socks.

Is it difficult to bury a mouse?
No, it's a small undertaking.

Did you hear about the mouse with pedestrian eyes? They look both ways before crossing.

'My mouse plays chess with me.'
'It must be very intelligent.'
'Not really, I've won two games so far.'

'I got involved in a narrow squeak.'
'What did you do?'
'I trod on a mouse.'

FRED: *Do you live in a small house?*
BERT: I should say. It's so small, even the mice
       are round shouldered.

'I understand you buried your pet mouse last
week?'
'I had to. He was dead.'

Did you hear about the mouse who dreamed he
was chewing his pillow? In the morning he was
all right, just a little down in the mouth.

We call our pet mouse Carpenter because he's
always doing little odd jobs around the house.

'My mouse died of flu.'
'But mice don't get flu.'
'Mine flew under a bus.'

'Do you serve mice?' asked the man in the pub.
'Of course we do, sir,' replied the barman.'
'Right then. A pint of beer for me and two mice
for my cat here.'

LADY CARRUTHERS: *Hudson, there is a mouse in the west drawing room.*

HUDSON: Very good, m'lady. I shall ascertain whether the cat is at home.

Did you hear about the baby mouse who saw a bat? He ran home and told his mother he'd seen an angel.

If 16 mice share a chocolate cake, what is the time?
A quarter to four.

If you keep watching Mickey Mouse films, what's up with you
You're having Disney spells.

In the fight between the hedgehog and the mouse, who won?
The hedgehog won on points.

Which cartoon character love sausages?
Meaty Mouse.

A woman dashed into a hardware shop and asked to be served at once. 'Quickly, get me a mousetrap,' she said. 'I've got a train to catch.'
'Sorry,' answered the assistant. 'We haven't got any as big as that.'

A man went into a bar and bet everyone there that he could prove that mice have three tails. 'Any mouse has more tails than no mouse, he said, 'and no mouse has two tails – so any mouse must have three tails.'
He won the bet!

Which mouse was Emperor of Rome?
Julius Cheeser.

OLD LADY: *My cat's getting too old to catch mice – I'd better have some tinned cat food.*
GROCER: Certainly, madam, what kind would you like?
OLD LADY: *Why, tinned mouse, of course!*

THE WOBBLY JELLY JOKE BOOK

Jim Eldridge

What car is like a sausage?
An old banger!

There was a man who had a blancmange in one ear and a jelly in the other.
He was a trifle deaf!

Here are jokes about everything from sausages, blancmange and custard to ice-cream and peas and jelly and cheese. A feast of fun that will have you in stitches from breakfast to teatime!